Radcliffe-

on old pictur

Pam Priestland

1. On the left of the road into Radcliffe from Nottingham stood Lamcote House. Built in the early years of the nineteenth century by Mr Topott, a Nottingham sugar confectioner, it was subsequently occupied by the Burnside and Birkin families. It was during the time of the Birkins in the 1920s that the Prince of Wales (later Edward VIII) was a frequent visitor to the house. Seen in its heyday on this "Clumber" series card, the house was eventually turned into flats and demolished in 1980, leaving only its wall and gateway to suggest former glory. The card was posted at Crown Hill in May 1907 with the message: *"We arrived safe last night. We were too late leaving Radcliffe to catch the proper train for Notts so we had to do a lot of shopping and landed here 10.30 p.m."*

Designed and Published by
Reflections of a Bygone Age,
Keyworth, Nottingham

1992

Printed by
Adlard Print and Typesetting Services,
Ruddington, Notts.

ISBN 0 946245 59 2

2. From the Lamcote end, Water Lane can now only be entered on foot, but before motor traffic enforced a one-way system, it was as much a central part of the village as Main Street. Early this century there were a number of small shops in the area, such as Brice's paint shop, shown here in the 1920s. Mrs Mary Brice is amongst the figures at the door.

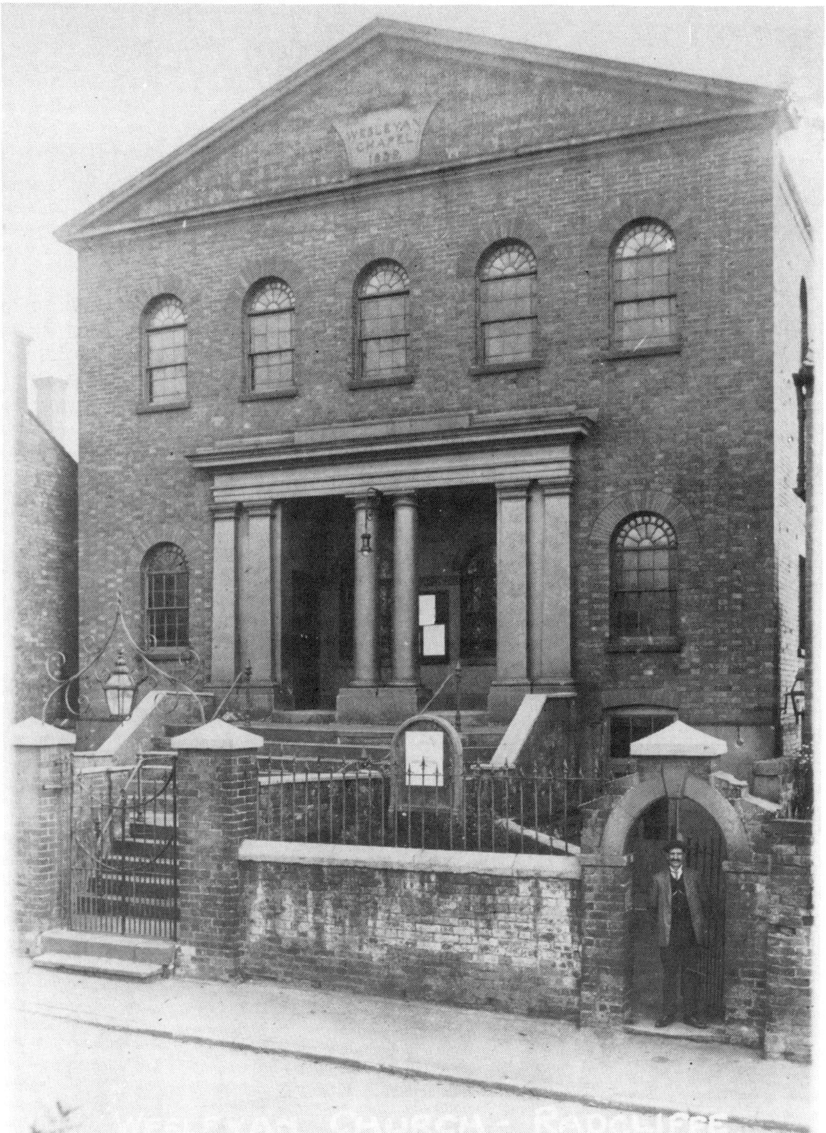

3. The Wesleyan Chapel on Mount Pleasant fronting the main road through the village. It was opened in 1839, replacing a smaller cottage building nearby. The figure in the gateway to the right is thought to be Mr Nowell, chapel keeper around the 1920s. The last services were held here in 1953, after which time they were transferred to the Primitive Methodist Chapel on Shelford Road. The building was demolished in 1967. This postcard is one of a number produced by Harold Taylor and was sent from Radcliffe in February 1914. *"I am starting from Radcliffe by the 9.40 train. As usual I shall be delighted for A to meet me. I am bringing the cycle so shall come round by Belvoir. Tell him to keep to the road."*

INTRODUCTION

By the early twentieth century, Radcliffe-on-Trent was fast losing its traditional agricultural image and becoming surburbanised. Such changes had begun slowly with the enclosure of the great open fields around 1789, thus allowing individuals to build houses away from the centre of the village. The process was accelerated by the coming of the railway in 1850. While reducing the importance of the river for trade, the railway widened the horizons of the villagers, and also brought Radcliffe within easy reach of Nottingham businessmen, particularly lace merchants, who preferred to live outside the city. From the 1880s substantial new houses near the station became much sought-after. Chestnut Grove, Shelford Road, Lorne Grove, Bingham Road and Cropwell Road in turn became lined with 'villas' staffed by resident servants. Advertisements boasted that the convenience of the railway meant that carriages no longer had to be maintained. At the other end of the scale, artisans' dwellings around Station Terrace, Victoria and Albert Streets or Sidney Grove became filled with workers who could also travel quickly and cheaply into Nottingham. This change in the village is reflected in the population increase from 761 in 1801 to 2093 in 1901. (In 1981 the population was 8215, the latest figures yet available).

The First World War brought other changes to the community, not least the significant losses in the male population. It also became impossible for Lord Manvers, the largest landowner in the village, to retain his hold. Much of the Manvers Estate was sold in 1920, again freeing further land for development. This changing world also saw the end of the 'gentry houses' of the village: Lamcote House and Cliff House have been demolished, Radcliffe Hall survives as the British Legion and Radcliffe Lodge is subdivided. Many of the old farmhouses in the centre of the village have been replaced by shops, although amongst the survivors are the Grange (now the Parish Council Offices), the Manor House and the Chestnuts (Rushleas), both as old people's homes. Motor transport, increasing from the 1920s and necessitating a by-pass in 1929, has confirmed the village as a suburb of Nottingham.

The postcards which follow are mainly from the first twenty years of the century, although some later ones have been included for comparison purposes. They are basically arranged in topographical rather than strictly chronological order, and follow a route as if approaching the village from the Lamcote (Nottingham) end.

Pam Priestland
September 1992

Acknowledgements: thanks for the loan of postcards to Tim Farr, Peter Cooke, Jeff Barratt, and Brian Lund.

Thanks, too, to Nottinghamshire Libraries for permission to use some cards from the extensive Fred Cutler collection of Radcliffe-on-Trent, which is housed in the local library.

Fuller information about the village's history can be found in
Radcliffe-on-Trent 1710-1837
Radcliffe-on-Trent 1837-1920

available from
ASHBRACKEN, 14 Cropwell Road, Radcliffe-on-Trent, Nottingham NG12 2FS

4. The Wesleyan Chapel football team for the 1922-3 season. The Rev Harold Baker is standing on the left, and standing second right is Noel Howard. Other figures have yet to be identified. Card published by un-named photographer.

5. The garden of Radcliffe Hall, now the British Legion, during the First World War. The Hall was used as a temporary hospital, and this card was sent by a Belgian patient to Belgian refugees on Cropwell Road in June 1915. The area is now partly occupied by Hall Close and Shadwell Grove.

6. St. Mary's Church, largely rebuilt in 1879 at the instigation of the Rev John Cullen, was a popular subject for postcards. This coloured view from about 1905 shows the saddle-back tower and clock, the latter a survival from the original building. The clock had been bought from William Pearce of Nottingham to commemorate the visit of Queen Victoria and Prince Albert to the village in December 1843. "Clumber" series card, posted from the village in October 1908: *"Came back by train yesterday."*

7. A similar view of the church and main road on a "Peveril" series postcard posted in August 1913. The Manvers Arms can be seen in the centre, while the chestnut trees lining the pavement on the left were formerly in the grounds of what was originally a farm until a road-widening scheme of 1911. The last of these chestnuts was removed in 1988 and new ones planted.

8. St. Mary's Church from the east end about 1903, with the saddle-back tower dominating the sky-line. According to local tradition, the unusual continental design of the tower was intended to remind the Rev John Cullen's German-born wife, Leontine, of home. Anonymously-published card posted in December 1903.

9. A coloured postcard written in 1906 showing the churchyard and beech trees in full leaf. The last burial in the churchyard was about 1870, from which time the cemetery in Vicarage Lane has been used. The large tree by the gate survived until 1989 when it was taken down. "Clumber" series, posted from Radcliffe in September 1906.

10. The church in winter in the early part of the century, giving a clear view of the triplet windows of the chancel and the side chapel. The rebuilding of the chancel area took place in 1858, some twenty years before the rest of the church, during the incumbency of the Rev. Robert Burgess. The creeper on the outside of the side chapel was subsequently removed. "Peveril" series postcard, posted at Nottingham in December 1906.

11. The unveiling of the War Memorial in St. Mary's churchyard in April 1921 by Colonel Charles Birkin of Lamcote House. The tall cross with the bowed figure of St. George bears the names of fifty-two Radcliffe men killed in the First World War, and nine who died as a result of illness on active service. The names of the dead of the Second World War have been added. The photograph was one of a number taken by Harold Taylor who ran a 'smallware' and draper's shop on Main Street and produced postcards as a sideline.

12. The interior of St. Mary's Church on a very early (1902) postard. Charles Bailey of Newark-on-Trent was the architect of the new chancel, side chapel and organ gallery in 1858 which had cost some £1,200. Goddard and Paget of Leicester designed the main rebuilding of 1879. For this, over £5,000 had been raised, largely from public donations.

13. Despite the rebuilding, fundraising was constantly necessary. For a Church Restoration project in 1924 a pageant was organised with participants congregating on a field at the side of Holme Lane. This was no.20 in the series of postcards commemorating the event.

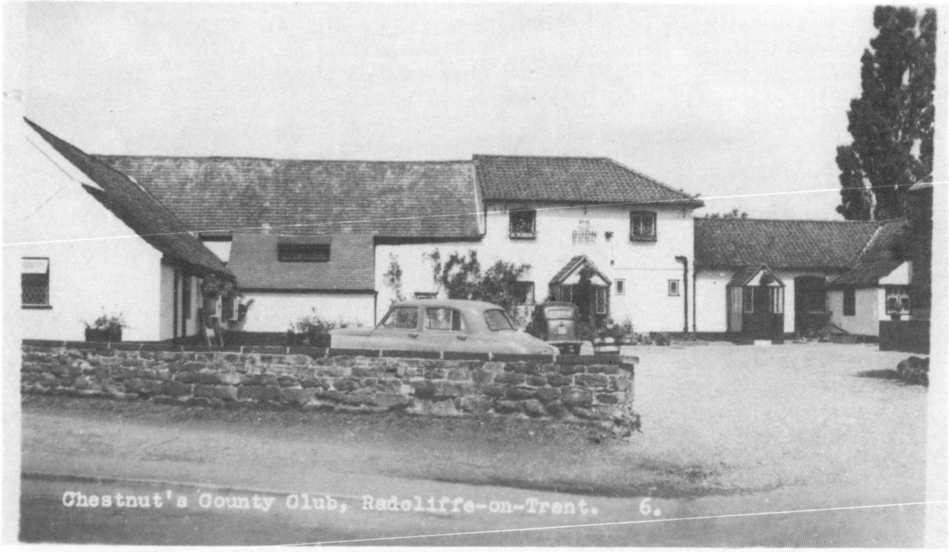

14. Across the road from the church, at one corner of Wharf Lane, was the Chestnuts, named after the trees which formerly stood in its grounds. Originally a farm, with its main building found on a map of 1710, it had become a Country Club run by Tom Brown by the time of this postcard of the 1960s. It has since been a restaurant and hotel, and is now an old people's home (Rushleas). The original name is preserved in the retirement homes on part of the site. The card was published by A.W. Bourne of Leicester.

15. Wharf Lane provided easy access to the River Trent. The Wharf House occupied by the wharfinger and ferryman is shown on this postcard from about 1905. It was built in 1820, replacing a previous building, and was once at the heart of a thriving trade in goods, notably coal and Crich lime, which were regularly landed at the wharf. This trade declined after the coming of the railway in 1850.

16. This "Clumber" series postcard shows the Wharf House (right) and the boat house (left) from the river side about 1910. The card bears a postmark for 1913. The railway bridge over Wharf Lane can be seen to the right, and the ferryman is in his boat.

17. A distant view of the wharf and ferry area. The figure in the boat is thought to be either George 'Trot' Upton, so-called because of a limp, who lived at the wharf for many years from the mid-1870s, or John Bell, who was ferryman around 1908. A single crossing cost a penny. The card is by the same publisher as the previous one.

18. Another view of the boat house and Wharf House early this century. The ferry boat is tied up on the bank, and smoke rises from the chimney of the small wash house used by the family living at the wharf. All these buildings have now been demolished and the area occupied by a caravan site. "Peveril" series real photographic card c.1910.

19. The importance of the ferry is emphasised by this card, in the same series as the previous one. It regularly took passengers across the Trent for Carlton, Colwick and Gedling, and the obligation to maintain it was a condition of sale when the remnants of the Manvers Estate were sold in 1941. The service has long since lapsed.

20. After Trot Upton and John Bell, Mrs Edna Vickerstaff was for many years the ferry keeper. Harold Taylor took the photograph for this card of her in the ferryboat c.1920.

21. Mrs Vickerstaff and children at the landing stage make a picturesque group on this postcard from a similar period, probably another Taylor publication.

22. The road down to the wharf in the 1930s with the Wharf House on the left, the small wash house in the centre, and the cliff on the right. A wooden 'cottage' (in the right foreground) stood close to the gateway of the present caravan site. This one is also by Taylor.

23. Apart from ferry boats, excursion and trading boats from Nottingham were once a common sight near Radcliffe. The photograph for this postcard was taken by Harold Taylor, probably in the 1920s, and shows the use of sail and steam. The barge in the foreground is the "Little John".

24. A postcard of cattle by the cliff and river at Radcliffe about 1910 emphasises that farming was the main occupation of the village until recent times. Old maps show that at one time cattle could be taken across shallow parts of the river to the Hesgang or Eastgang pasture on the other side which then belonged to the village. It became part of Stoke Bardolph parish around the time of the First World War.

25. Many visitors came to Radcliffe from Victorian times onwards, and the walk above the cliffs was one of the attractions. A solitary figure surveys the winding River Trent in the 1920s from the Malkin Hill area. Cliff House, now demolished and the site covered by Oak Tree Avenue, was behind the spectator. The view looks across towards Stoke Bardolph and Burton Joyce. The ferry point was to the left.

26. A mother and child climb up the cliff path above the river on this postcard from the late 1920s. Although this was always a popular area, permanent access was only acquired for the village through the generosity of Lisle Rockley as part of the memorial to his son killed in the First World War.

27. A postcard sent from Radcliffe in November 1906, the trees lining the cliff and adjacent path from about the time the area was given permanently to the village by Lisle Rockley.

28. The Rockley Memorial Park at the top of the cliff shortly after it was opened by Viscount Galway in 1927. The summer house carries an inscription explaining that Lisle Rockley's gift was in memory of the men of the parish who fell in the Great War, and especially of his only son, Lieut. William Lisle Rockley, M.C. of the 10th York and Lancaster Regiment, who was killed at Ypres. The work of clearing and planting was carried out as far as possible by ex-servicemen. The park has recently been replanted (1992). This card was posted in September 1935, with another reference to the 'last train' in the message.

29. On the village corner of Wharf Lane stands the Manor House. A "Clumber" postcard from about 1906 shows it on the left next to the 'Manvers Arms'. With a seventeenth century core, the Manor House has had many additions and is now a retirement home for the frail and elderly. At the time of the photograph it was occupied by the Dowson family, but, like the 'Manvers Arms', was owned by the Manvers Estate until 1920.

30. Another view of the 'Manvers Arms' about 1920. Originally the 'White Hart', it was rebuilt by the Manvers Estate around 1815, using a basic design by William Wilkins found in other Estate architecture at Budby, Cotgrave and Holme Pierrepont. The Bell family were the landlords from 1817 until 1920. Beyond the inn can be seen Richmond House and farm, the latter now a garden supplies and pet shop.

31. The centre of Radcliffe, looking towards the corner of Shelford Road about 1918. On the left can be seen Parr's butcher's shop, and the Post Office block. In the centre is the Co-operative Stores, built around 1902 to replace the original stores opened on Hogg Lane in 1874. To the right can be seen the horse trough and drinking fountain unveiled in 1902 to commemorate the coronation of Edward VII. The card was sent to Belgium: *"Thanks for the postcards which I was pleased to have."*

32. At the corner of Shelford Road, opposite the Co-operative stores, was the wooden cabin shown on this postcard from the early years of the century, occupied by Thomas Barratt, boot and shoemaker. His assistants shown here were his son, Donald Barratt, and Jack Cragg. In more recent times the cabin was Astill's sweet shop. It still stands, but is now brick clad.

33. Radcliffe-on-Trent railway station still serves passengers on the Nottingham-Grantham line as it did in 1913 on this "Peveril" postcard. Then the first train of the morning on the Great Northern line to Nottingham (Victoria) left at 5.16 a.m. In the other direction it was possible to travel to both Grantham and Melton Mowbray (via Bingham Road). *"I shall come home today. I am enjoying myself very much. The weather has been lovely,"* wrote Gladys from Radcliffe in August 1913.

34. Once over the railway bridge early this century, the left side of Shelford Road consisted mainly of fields. This postcard from 1904 shows an informal game of cricket - the players mainly female - taking place in Bridge Field. The site is now occupied by Fernwood Drive and Oak Tree Avenue.

35. Shelford Road remained comparatively rural between the wars as is shown by the lack of street lights and by the children playing in the roadway on this postcard from 1924. The houses between Cliff Way and Park Road were built shortly after the First World War by the Rural District Housing Committee.

36. Back in the village centre, horse-drawn charabancs wait with excursionists beside the horse trough and drinking fountain on Whit Monday 1912. The trees of the 'Grange' and the corner of Vicarage Lane can be seen in the background.

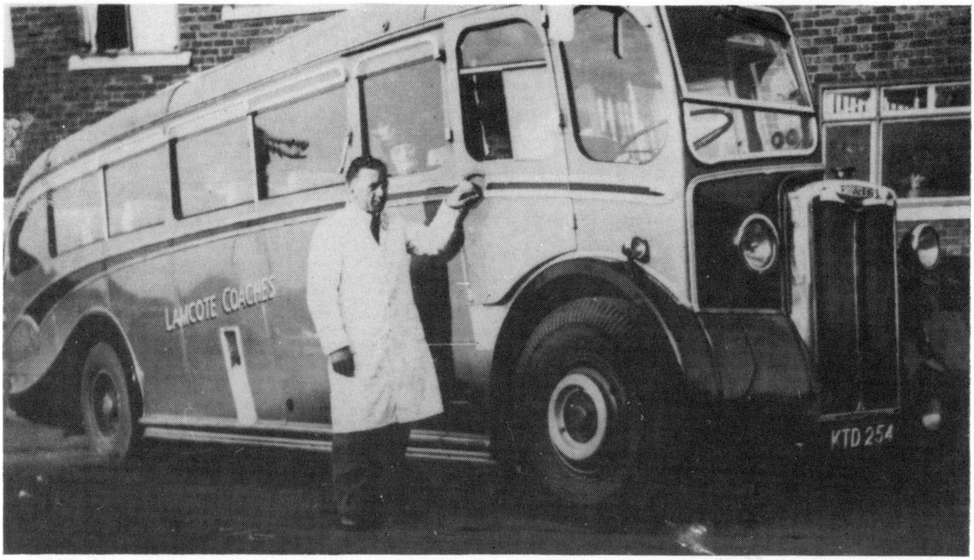

37. From the 1920s, holiday outings were often by motorised transport. Lamcote Motors was started in 1946, and from the 1950s (the date of this postcard) their coaches were to become a familiar sight in Radcliffe.

38. A postcard from about 1930 showing the Co-operative Stores on the left. The upper floor was used as assembly rooms. It was replaced by the present flat-roofed building in the 1960s. Across the road can be seen the gateway to the 'Grange' (originally a farm, then used for private residence before being acquired by the Parish Council in 1975). Beyond the Co-op the distinctive roof of the Police Station stands above the adjacent buildings.

39. Looking in the same direction along the main street towards Bingham Road in 1919, this postcard shows the Peace Celebrations of that year. The original photograph was taken out of the upper window of Harold Taylor's draper's shop, the sign of the adjacent 'Black Lion' inn being caught in the upper left corner. The lady pushing the pram has been identified as Mrs Speed.

40. Postcards of the Main Street looking towards Bingham Road in the 1960s show a number of changes from today. Banking, originally carried out in part of the Co-operative building, had become a prominent part of village life. The National Provincial Bank shown on the left became the National Westminster in 1970. Rowe's newsagents became County News in 1991. The Police Station, then still in use, stood next to Rowe's garage which had replaced a farm, and was itself soon to be demolished and replaced by Kingston Court and three shops. Card published by A.W. Bourne.

41. Further along Main Street in the 1960s can be seen the draper's shop run by Harold Taylor's son, Alvyn (later Mayor of Rushcliffe and Chairman of the Parish Council), the third generation of the family to run the business. A Victorian fire insurance plate is in the blocked upper window. After the business was sold in 1984, the window was opened up. Onions' butcher's shop next door was formerly the 'Black Lion' Inn, and the three adjacent shops at the corner of Station Terrace were built in the inn garden. The house at the corner of New Road was 'Hollybank', which became a social club about 1925, and was demolished in 1973 to make way for more shops. Another Bourne card.

42. A number of postcards show Main Street over the years looking back towards the church. Compare this view with illus. 43. Here a public telephone box has been erected. The card was published by a London firm around 1935. The first private telephone in the village, incidentally, was in Bailey Lane, and in 1907 the National Telephone Company had an exchange at 20 Bingham Road. It was taken over by the Post Office in 1913.

43. An earlier view on a "Rex" series postcard of the early 1920s. Motorised transport was becoming more common, although the delivery boy was still on foot. On the right was Barratt's Post Office, the letter box being then in the wall. Parr's butchers, with blinds above the window, was next door. The adjacent garden is now occupied by the town houses of Parr's Court.

MAIN ROAD
RADCLIFFE ON TRENT
REX SERIES 453.

44. Moving further along Main Street, this postcard, from 1905, emphasises the use of horse-drawn vehicles and bicycles, rather than motorised transport. On the right is the Police Station in its heyday. Built in 1875 to combat the disorderliness of the numerous visitors who came to the village, it contained a lock-up and living accommodation. The Co-operative Stores can be seen at the corner of Shelford Road.

45. This view from a similar period shows the corner of the 'Royal Oak' Inn across the road from the Police Station. Beyond the inn is Kyte's the Chemist (said to be where all the flies went in the winter time) at the corner of Richmond Terrace. Next to the Police Station is the farmhouse then occupied by Elvira Bowring. It was to be replaced by Rowe's garage.

46. Rowe's garage, which replaced Elvira Bowring's farmhouse, on a postcard from 1935. The site is now occupied by Kingston Court and three shops. Flowering trees fill the gardens at the corner of Bolton Terrace. Notice the traffic scars in the Main Street.

47. The garden wall of the original 'Black Lion' at the corner of Station Terrace can clearly be seen in this card from 1905. (The bar from which the inn sign hangs is still in place, although the premises have long been used as a butcher's shop). A man sits on a weighing machine alongside the wall. Next to the inn can be seen the draper's shop run by the Taylor family from the 1880s until 1984.

48. Village children line up across the street outside the 'Black Lion'. Beyond the out-houses on the left at the corner of Walker's Yard can be seen Dunmore House, then the residence of Dr Archibald Campbell. The site is now occupied by a supermarket. "Clumber" series postcard, sent in April 1914, but published about nine years earlier.

49. Dunmore House on the Bank Holiday of August 7th 1922 when Radcliffe was flooded. This was an extreme version of a number of floods recorded from Victorian times onwards, partly caused by the inability of the Syke Drain (a now-culverted stream lying under much of the Main Street) to cope with excessive rain. Notable flooding also occured in 1936, 1947 and 1967.

50. A view looking towards Bingham Road from outside the 'Black Lion' Inn about 1915 when Frederick W. Platts was the licensee. The corner of Station Terrace can be seen on the left, and George Henry Buxton's farm on the right, reaching to the corner of Cropwell Road. This was eventually to be replaced by a new 'Black Lion'.

51. It was in 1928 that the licence from the 'Black Lion' on the Main Street was transferred to the large new building at the corner of Cropwell Road, built on the site of Buxton's farm and the village pinfold. It is shown here on a postcard from the 1960s, published by Bourne.

52. Developments on Cropwell Road itself largely began in the 1880s as the building boom encouraged by the arrival of the railway spread beyond the immediate vicinity of the station. This postcard by Harold Taylor in the 1920s shows the corner of 25 Cropwell Road (originally the 'Hollies') and houses on either side of Albert Street. The railings were subsequently removed in the 1939-45 war effort. In the distance can be seen the fields now occupied by New Road.

53. In the opposite direction, Cropwell Road houses were more isolated, particularly beyond the by-pass (built in 1929). The view on this 1920s postcard shows the House on the Hill in the distance on the left, and Millfield House on the right.

54. New schools were built on Cropwell Road in the 1960s. This Bourne postcard late in that decade shows the Secondary School which became Dayncourt Comprehensive School in 1972. The totem pole at the entrance was a gift from the Canadian airmen who lived on the Canadian estate in the village in the 1950s.

55. At the junction with Cropwell Road, the village Main Street merges into Bingham Road. This "Clumber" postcard from 1905 shows few changes from the scene today, although the house behind the tree at the corner of Lorne Grove was demolished in the 1960s and replaced by Hazard's grocer's shop; it is now a furniture suppliers.

56. A subsequent addition to the corner of Bingham Road was Cyril Rose's garage. The business was begun in the 1920s and is shown on this postcard in 1952. In the background can be seen Lynton House, the first house (c.1870) to be built in Lorne Grove.

57. Lorne Grove (named after the Marquess of Lorne who married Queen Victoria's daughter in 1871) developed as the railway brought easy access for Nottingham businessmen who wished to live out of the city. This postcard by Harold Taylor in about 1912 looks towards the outlet to the station at the top. Note the gas lamp.

58. Typical houses in Lorne Grove are numbers 9 and 11, shown here on a postcard sent in the 1920s. The Cliftons and the Barratts were the occupants of the two houses at that time.

59. Local builders had benefitted from Radcliffe's expansion in the late nineteenth and early twentieth centuries. One such was William Vickerstaff, shown here shortly before his death in May 1914 at the age of 68, with his patient pony. In 1881, when living on Bailey Lane, he had employed as many as sixteen men.

60. Multi-view postcards of the village became popular from the 1920s, some incorporating much older photographs. This card was posted in 1922, and shows clockwise from the left:the ferry house and wharf; Holme Pierrepont Hall; the river and ferry boat; St. Mary's Church; and (centre) a 1905 view of the Main Street looking towards the church from the Police Station.